TOUGH QUESTIONS

QUESTIONS

REVISED EDITION

HOW RELIABLE IS THE BIBLE?

The Tough Questions Series

TOUGH
QUESTIONS
REVISED EDITION

HOW

RELIABLE

IS THE

BIBLE?

HOW RELIABLE IS THE BIBLE?

JUDSON POLING
foreword by **Lee Strobel**

WILLOW
CREEK
RESOURCES

ZONDERVAN™

GRAND RAPIDS, MICHIGAN 49530 USA

We want to hear from you. Please send your comments about this book to us in care of zreview@zondervan.com. Thank you.

ZONDERVAN™

How Reliable Is the Bible?
Copyright © 1998, 2003 by Willow Creek Association

Requests for information should be addressed to:

Zondervan, *Grand Rapids, Michigan 49530*

ISBN: 0-310-24504-4

Interior design by Nancy Wilson

Printed in the United States of America

04 05 06 07 08 09 /❖ CH/ 10 9 8 7 6 5 4 3 2

Contents

Foreword

For most of my life I was an atheist. I thought that the Bible was hopelessly riddled with mythology, that God was a man-made creation born of wishful thinking, and that the deity of Jesus was merely a product of legendary development. My no-nonsense education in journalism and law contributed to my skeptical viewpoint. In fact, just the idea of an all-powerful, all-loving, all-knowing creator of the universe seemed too absurd to even justify the time to investigate whether there could be any evidence backing it up.

However, my agnostic wife's conversion to Christianity, and the subsequent transformation of her character and values, prompted me to launch my own spiritual journey in 1980. Using the skills I developed as the legal affairs editor of *The Chicago Tribune,* I began to check out whether any concrete facts, historical data, or convincing logic supported the Christian faith. Looking back, I wish I had this curriculum to supplement my efforts.

This excellent material can help you in two ways. If you're already a Christ-follower, this series can provide answers to some of the tough questions your seeker friends are asking—or you're asking yourself. If you're not yet following Christ but consider yourself either an open-minded skeptic or a spiritual seeker, this series can also help you in your journey. You can thoroughly and responsibly explore the relevant issues while discussing the topics in community with others. In short, it's a tremendous guide for people who really want to discover the truth about God and this fascinating and challenging Nazarene carpenter named Jesus.

If the previous paragraph describes you in some way, prepare for the adventure of a lifetime. Let the pages that follow take you on a stimulating journey of discovery as you grapple with the most profound—and potentially life-changing—questions in the world.

—Lee Strobel, author of
The Case for Christ and *The Case for Faith*

Getting Started

Welcome to the Tough Questions series! This small group curriculum was produced with the conviction that claims regarding spiritual truth can and should be tested. Religions—sometimes considered exempt from scrutiny—are not free to make sweeping declarations and demands without providing solid reasons why they should be taken seriously. These teachings, including those from the Bible in particular, purport to explain the most significant of life's mysteries, with consequences alleged to be eternal. Such grand claims should be analyzed carefully. If this questioning process exposes faulty assertions, it only makes sense to refuse to place one's trust in these flawed systems of belief. If, on the other hand, an intense investigation leads to the discovery of truth, the search will have been worth it all.

Christianity contends that God welcomes sincere examination and inquiry; in fact, it's a matter of historical record that Jesus encouraged such scrutiny. The Bible is not a secret kept only for the initiated few, but an open book available for study and debate. The central teachings of Christianity are freely offered to all, to the skeptic as well as to the believer.

So here's an open invitation: explore the options, examine the claims, and draw your conclusions. And once you encounter and embrace the truth—look out! Meaningful life-change and growth will be yours to enjoy.

It is possible for any of us to believe error; it is also feasible for us to resist truth. Using this set of discussion guides will help you sort out the true from the supposed, and ultimately offer a reasonable defense of the Christian faith. Whether you are a nonbeliever or

> You will seek me and find me when you seek me with all your heart.
>
> —Jeremiah 29:13

9

skeptic, or someone who is already convinced and looking to fortify your faith, these guides will lead you to a fascinating exploration of vital spiritual truths.

Tough Questions for Small Groups

The Tough Questions series is specifically designed to give spiritual seekers (or non-Christians) a chance to raise questions and investigate the basics of the Christian faith within the safe context of a seeker small group. These groups typically consist of a community of two to twelve seekers and one or two leaders who gather on a regular basis, primarily to discuss spiritual matters. Seeker groups meet at a wide variety of locations, from homes and offices to restaurants and churches to bookstores and park district picnic tables. A trained Christian leader normally organizes the group and facilitates the discussions based on the seekers' spiritual concerns and interests. Usually, at least one apprentice (or coleader) who is also a Christian assists the group leader. The rest of the participants are mostly, if not all, non-Christians. This curriculum is intended to enhance these seeker small group discussions and create a fresh approach to exploring the Christian faith.

Because the primary audience is the not-yet-convinced seeker, these guides are designed to represent the skeptical, along with the Christian, perspective. While the truths of the Christian position are strongly affirmed, it is anticipated that non-Christians will dive into these materials with a group of friends and discover that their questions and doubts are not only well understood and represented here, but also valued. If that goal is accomplished, open and honest discussions about Christianity can follow. The greatest hope behind the formation of this series is that seekers will be challenged in a respectful way to seriously consider and even accept the claims of Christ.

A secondary purpose behind the design of this series is to provide a tool for small groups of Christians to use as they discuss answers to the tough questions seekers are asking. The process of wrestling through these important questions and issues will not only strengthen their own personal faith but also provide them with insights for entering into informed dialogues about Christianity with their seeking friends.

A hybrid of the two options mentioned above may make more sense for some groups. For example, a small group of Christians may want to open up their discussion to include those who are just beginning to investigate spiritual things. This third approach provides an excellent opportunity for both Christians and seekers to examine the claims of Christianity together. Whatever the configuration of your group, may you benefit greatly as you use these guides to fully engage in lively discussions about issues that matter most.

Guide Features

The Introduction

At the beginning of every session is an introduction, usually several paragraphs long. You may want to read this beforehand even though your leader will probably ask the group to read it aloud together at the start of every meeting. These introductions are written from a skeptical point of view, so a full spectrum of perspectives is represented in each session. Hopefully, this information will help you feel represented, understood, and valued.

Open for Discussion

Most sessions contain ten to fifteen questions your group can discuss. You may find that it is difficult for your group to get through all these questions in one sitting. That is okay; the important thing is to engage in the topic at hand—not to necessarily get through every question. Your group, however, may decide to spend more than one meeting on each session in order to address all of the questions. The Open for Discussion sections are designed to draw out group participation and give everyone the opportunity to process things openly.

Usually, the first question of each session is an "icebreaker." These simple questions are designed to get the conversation going by prompting the group to discuss a nonthreatening issue, usually having to do with the session topic to be covered. Your group may want to make time for additional icebreakers at the beginning of each discussion.

Heart of the Matter

The section called "Heart of the Matter" represents a slight turn in the group discussion. Generally speaking, the questions in this section speak more to the emotional, rather than just the intellectual, side of the issue. This is an opportunity to get in touch with how you feel about a certain aspect of the topic being discussed and to share those feelings with the rest of the group.

Charting Your Journey

The purpose of the "Charting Your Journey" section is to challenge you to go beyond a mere intellectual and emotional discussion to personal application. This group experience is, after all, a journey, so each session includes this section devoted to helping you identify and talk about your current position. Your views will most likely fluctuate as you make new discoveries along the way.

Straight Talk

Every session has at least one section, called "Straight Talk," designed to stimulate further thinking and discussion around relevant supplementary information. The question immediately following Straight Talk usually refers to the material just presented, so it is important that you read and understand this part before you attempt to answer the question.

Quotes

Scattered throughout every session are various quotes, many of them from skeptical or critical points of view. These are simply intended to spark your thinking about the issue at hand.

Recommended Resources

This section at the back of each guide lists recommended books that may serve as helpful resources for further study.

Discussion Guidelines

These guides, which consist mainly of questions to be answered in your group setting, are designed to elicit dialogue rather than short, simple answers. Strictly speaking, these guides are not Bible studies, though they regularly refer to biblical themes and passages. Instead, they are topical discussion guides, meant to get you talking about what you really think and feel. The sessions have a point and attempt to lead to some resolution, but they fall short of providing the last word on any of the questions raised. That is left for you to discover for yourself! You will be invited to bring your experience, perspective, and uncertainties to the discussion, and you will also be encouraged to compare your beliefs with what the Bible teaches in order to determine where you stand as each meeting unfolds.

Your group should have a discussion leader. This facilitator can get needed background material for each session in the *Tough Questions Leader's Guide*.

There, your leader will find some brief points of clarification and understanding (along with suggested answers) for many of the questions in each session. The supplemental book *Seeker Small Groups* is also strongly recommended as a helpful resource for leaders to effectively start up small groups and facilitate discussions for spiritual seekers. *The Complete Book of Questions: 1001 Conversation Starters for Any Occasion,* a resource filled with icebreaker questions, may be a useful tool to assist everyone in your group to get to know one another better, and to more easily launch your interactions.

In addition, keep the following list of suggestions in mind as you prepare to participate in your group discussions.

1. The Tough Questions series does not necessarily need to be discussed sequentially. The guides, as well as individual sessions, can be mixed and matched in any order and easily discussed independently of each other, based on everyone's interests and questions.

2. If possible, read over the material before each meeting. Familiarity with the topic will greatly enrich the time you spend in the group discussion.

3. Be willing to join in the group interaction. The leader of the group will not present a lecture but rather will encourage each of you to openly discuss your opinions and disagreements. Plan to share your ideas honestly and forthrightly.

4. Be sensitive to the other members of your group. Listen attentively when they speak and be affirming whenever you can. This will encourage more hesitant members of the group to participate. Always remember to show respect toward the others even if they don't always agree with your position.

5. Be careful not to dominate the discussion. By all means participate, but allow others to have equal time.
6. Try to stick to the topic being studied. There won't be enough time to handle the peripheral tough questions that come to mind during your meeting.
7. It would be helpful for you to have a good modern translation of the Bible, such as the New International Version, the New Living Translation, or the New American Standard Bible. You might prefer to use a Bible that includes notes especially for seekers, such as *The Journey: The Study Bible for Spiritual Seekers.* Unless noted otherwise, questions in this series are based on the New International Version.
8. Do some extra reading in the Bible and other recommended books as you work through these sessions. The "Recommended Resources" section at the back of each guide offers some ideas of books to read.

Unspeakable Love

Christianity stands or falls on Christ. Yet he left us with a whole lot of hard sayings. But the central scandal of Christianity is that at a point in history, God came down to live among us in a person, Jesus of Nazareth. And the most baffling moment of Jesus' life was on the cross, where he hung to die like a common criminal. In that place of weakness—where all seemed lost, where the taunts of "Prove yourself, Jesus, and come down from there!" lashed out like the whip that flogged him prior to his crucifixion—somehow God was at his best. There at the cross, he expressed a love greater than words could ever describe. That act of Jesus, presented as the ultimate demonstration of the love and justice of God, begs to be put to "cross" examination.

As you wrestle with these tough questions, be assured that satisfying, reasonable answers are waiting to be found. And you're invited to discover them with others in your small group as you explore and discuss these guides. God bless you on your spiritual journey!

Seek and you will find; knock and the door will be opened to you.

—Matthew 7: 7

How Reliable
Is the Bible?

They were about the nicest young men you'd want to meet. They came to the door and politely introduced themselves as representatives of the Church of Jesus Christ of Latter-day Saints. They claimed that God had given the world additional scripture, namely the Book of Mormon, which they offered free. When asked what credentials this book held to support their assertion, they gave their standard reply: "If you pray about it and ask the Holy Spirit to tell you if this book is from God, he will show you personally. Read it and find out." Archaeological research was unnecessary, historical inquiry not needed—just a direct word from God and you'd know.

On the other side of the world, devout Muslims believe that the Koran was divinely dictated by God to the prophet Mohammed early in the seventh century A.D. Word for word, Allah spoke his revelations through the archangel, and they were written down, preserved for the world to receive. The original Koran exists in heaven, because it is the uncreated eternal Word of God; the earthly Koran is a mere copy. For a Muslim to question the Koran's accuracy or truthfulness is a grave sin, for the faithful must believe and not doubt.

The same is true for the Bible, right? God revealed it and we are all supposed to accept it on faith. Take a biblical Christian, a Muslim, and a Mormon and lock them in a room, and each would try to get the others to accept his book as the true revelation of

God's Word. But if you, as an unbiased seeker of truth, were locked in that room with them, what would you conclude? Each religion's representative seems to be telling you to accept his, with no further proof than "You'll know once you read it." How would you know which book, if any, was the truthful one?

Some say prayer or subjective experience is not enough to solve such a ticklish problem. Religious books, like any other history or wisdom literature, should be examined and tested. Any inaccuracy in things measurable, like historical details, undermines accuracy in things spiritual, such as the claim that the book's message will save you eternally.

You may come to the point where you reject all books that claim to be the Word of God. Mark Twain called the Book of Mormon "chloroform in print" and found fault with the Bible and the Koran as well. Robert Ingersoll was even more biting in his criticism of the Bible's message; in his opinion, "If a man would follow, today, the teachings of the Old Testament, he would be a criminal. If he would follow strictly the teachings of the New, he would be insane."

What evidence is there that the Bible is trustworthy, more so than any other sacred scripture? Does it have any credentials that compel us to take it seriously? Or will the Bible's teaching lead to criminal and insane behavior, as Ingersoll predicted?

These are not merely academic questions. What's at stake is whether God has spoken to us through the written word, and where that message is located.

It is of course possible that God has not spoken (as it is possible that there is no God to speak!). But it is claimed that he has spoken, and those claims deserve a hearing—which requires careful investigation. This series of discussions will help you get an answer to the question "How reliable is the Bible?" so you can make up your own mind.

Where Did the Bible Come From?

Primary Source?

When you go to the bookstore and head over to the religion section, you will undoubtedly find Bibles—lots of Bibles. The assortment of translations and sheer volume of choices may overwhelm you.

Believers claim that the Bible is God's book—or at a minimum, an important book about God. In light of such an audacious claim, one of the first questions raised is, "Where did the Bible come from?" We know it didn't drop down from heaven complete with leather cover and gilded pages. In fact, it didn't drop down from heaven at all, even as a rough draft. People wrote it. Human beings like you and me. Who were these people? Why did they write? When did they write it? And how do we know they were right about what they wrote?

Sometimes people will buy a Bible for a friend, and that person, out of curiosity, starts reading. Imagine you are someone who knows almost nothing about the Bible. What would be your first reaction as you perused its pages? Would you be able to make heads or tails out of it? What features would surprise you—or baffle you?

One of the first things that would stand out is the human quality of the writings. If you were expecting the Bible to be the Word of God, you would probably be expecting the words of God—maybe something

All Bibles are man-made.

—Thomas Edison

like a transcription of God's sermons. There should be commandments, pronouncements, even judgments—all with quotation marks as something God said to someone.

Yet the first words of the Bible are, "In the beginning God created the heavens and the earth." God is spoken of in the third person. These are the words of a man saying what God did, not God saying what he did. This is true for most of the Bible; the writers seem to record their own words and commentary mixed in with direct quotes from God.

There are many more questions you might have. Are we supposed to believe that the people who wrote the Bible should be taken literally? And when they do quote God, did he say something out loud that they could hear? If so, how did they know it was God talking and not a demon? If it wasn't an audible voice but only an impression in their minds, how did they know it was God and not their subconscious? Why should we believe their inner impressions of what God supposedly said any more than our own?

Then we must ask, how did these writings come together in one volume? Who did the picking and choosing? What if they overlooked some book that God wanted included? What if they included something with errors? What if this whole business of a book from God is just presumption—a mere human asserting he knows for sure what God said? The origin of this supposed book from God raises many tough questions. Get ready for some lively discussion!

OPEN FOR DISCUSSION

1. What do you remember hearing or believing about the Bible as you were growing up? Were you an "easy sell" or did you tend to be skeptical about its contents?

The Bible is a book that has been read more and examined less than any book that ever existed.

—*The Theological Works of Thomas Paine*

2. What nagging doubts about the Bible do you have now? If the sessions in this guide could answer one question for you, what would that be?

STRAIGHT TALK

Unexpected Revelation

Imagine for a minute that you were God and you wanted to communicate with humankind through a book. Wouldn't the simplest thing be to get someone to take down your words — a prophet or scribe of some kind — and then have that person publish your collected sayings? To many people, that seems to make the most sense. When those folks open the Bible for the first time, that's what they expect to find.

Yet the Bible is surprisingly not like that at all. It is full of history, told from the point of view of those who experienced it. It contains, of all things, genealogies — lists of names of who begat whom — and various other seemingly irrelevant details. True, there are places where a prophet speaks for God, and those words are recorded with the characteristic "Thus says the Lord," but particulars of the prophet's life and experiences are also written down.

When we come to the part of the Bible that's about Jesus, we have not only a record of his words but also a record of the words of those he talked to (even his enemies), as well as accounts of his deeds. Clearly, the Gospels are more than just quotes from Jesus. The letters that make up a third of the New

DISCUSSION ONE

21

Testament are the words of men such as the apostle Paul or Peter, leaders who are trying to encourage and teach the people in the churches with which they've worked. So while there are the "sayings of God" in the Bible, there are apparently many "sayings of men," too.

3. Do you think there's any value in having more than just "dictated pronouncements from God" in the Bible? Explain. When the biblical writers include details about themselves or others, how does this enhance what God supposedly said and did in their lives?

STRAIGHT TALK

Who Wrote the Bible?

The Bible is not just one book — it is a collection of dozens of books. Yet all these writings taken together speak with unity and proclaim unmistakably, "People matter to God!"

- It was written over a period of fourteen hundred years.
- It was written over a span of forty generations.
- It was written by over forty authors from all walks of life (kings, peasants, philosophers, poets, fishermen, statesmen, scholars, doctors, businessmen, etc.).
- It was written on three continents (Asia, Africa, Europe), in many different places (dungeons, palaces, while traveling, the wilderness, etc.).
- It was written during a variety of moods (sorrow, joy, anger, excitement, tranquillity).
- It was written in three languages (Hebrew, Aramaic, Greek).

4. What might be the disadvantages of having so many authors put together a book? How might this process add value to the end result?

STRAIGHT TALK

What Makes These Writings So Special?

None of the biblical writers claimed to be anything other than mortal men, yet they insisted they were God's instruments. They believed they wrote accurate history, preserved accurate eyewitness accounts, had accurate revelations from God, and made accurate predictions about the future.

Accurate History

Many have undertaken to draw up an account of the things that have been fulfilled among us, just as they were handed down to us by those who from the first were eyewitnesses and servants of the word. Therefore, since I myself have carefully investigated everything from the beginning, it seemed good also to me to write an orderly account for you, most excellent Theophilus, so that you may know the certainty of the things you have been taught.

—Luke 1:1–4

Accurate Eyewitness Accounts

We did not follow cleverly invented stories when we told you about the power and coming of our Lord Jesus Christ, but we were eyewitnesses of his majesty. For he received honor and glory from God the Father when the voice came to him from the Majestic Glory, saying, "This is my Son, whom I love; with him I am well pleased." We ourselves heard this voice that came from heaven when we were with him on the sacred mountain.

— 2 Peter 1:16–18

Accurate Revelation from God

Above all, you must understand that no prophecy of Scripture came about by the prophet's own interpretation. For prophecy never had its origin in the will of man, but men spoke from God as they were carried along by the Holy Spirit.

— 2 Peter 1:20–21

Accurate Predictions About the Future

I foretold the former things long ago, my mouth announced them and I made them known; then suddenly I acted, and they came to pass. For I knew how stubborn you were. . . . Therefore I told you these things long ago; before they happened I announced them to you so that you could not say, "My idols did them; my wooden image and metal god ordained them." You have heard these things; look at them all. Will you not admit them?

— Isaiah 48:3–6

---

5. It's one thing to say God is speaking through you, and another thing to substantiate it. What kind of validation would need to be provided by someone who claims to be giving us ultimate truth?

Who Picked the Books to Be Included and Why?

The Old Testament books were accepted by a group of Jewish scholars in the city of Jamnia in A.D. 90, though the books they ratified were widely circulated before then. The Old Testament, originally written in Hebrew, had been translated into Greek around the third century B.C. because Greek was the more common language spoken. In Jesus' day the Old Testament was referred to as the Law, the Prophets, and the Writings (or more commonly just the Law and the Prophets). This designation referred to the same books that are in our Old Testament today.

Jesus repeatedly validated the Old Testament as a whole: "Do not think that I have come to abolish the Law or the Prophets; I have not come to abolish them but to fulfill them" (Matthew 5:17). He even seemed to indicate the beginning and end points of the Old Testament by referring to an event in Genesis and then another in 2 Chronicles (Matthew 23:35) — the first and last books according to the Hebrew order. He considered these the "bookends" of divine Jewish revelation.

The New Testament books were all written before the end of the first century and were widely circulated as individual books for several centuries. The first list of all the New Testament books together as we find them in our Bibles today was written in A.D. 367 by Athanasius. Other partial lists existed before then, but his list and the Councils of Hippo (A.D. 393) and Carthage (A.D. 397 and 419) formalized the New Testament as it's come down to us today.

6. What safeguards are inherent in a centuries-long process of confirming the books of the Bible?

7. If someone came today and said they had a book of truth that should be included in the Bible, what criteria would you use for evaluating their claim?

STRAIGHT TALK

Evaluating a Prophet

In the Old Testament, the people of Israel were given ways to test a prophet. Any person who claimed he was speaking truth from God had to be evaluated. If the person failed either of the following qualifications, he and his message were to be disregarded.

The first qualification was whether the prophet's message contained absolutely accurate predictions.

> You may say to yourselves, "How can we know when a message has not been spoken by the Lord?" If what a prophet proclaims in the name of the Lord does not take place or come true, that is a message the Lord has not spoken. That prophet has spoken presumptuously. Do not be afraid of him.
>
> — Deuteronomy 18:21–22

The second qualification was whether the prophet's message contained absolutely accurate theology.

> If a prophet, or one who foretells by dreams, appears among you and announces to you a miraculous sign or wonder, and if the sign or wonder of which he has spoken takes place, and he says, "Let us follow other gods" (gods you have not known) "and let us worship them," you must not listen to the words of that prophet or dreamer. The Lord your God is testing you to find out whether you love him with all your heart and with all your soul. It is the Lord your God you must follow, and him you must revere. Keep his commands and obey him; serve him and hold fast to him.
>
> — Deuteronomy 13:1–4

8. Even if a modern-day psychic had a ninety percent accuracy rate, would he or she pass the first test above? How would this test rate a prophet like Joseph Smith of the Latter-day Saints (Mormons), who made several prophecies that never came true—even though he made some that did?

9. What would the second test, of theological accuracy, do to many who claim prophetic messages today and even appear to have miraculous powers, yet teach unbiblical theology?

HEART OF THE MATTER

10. What is troublesome to you about believing that the Bible is the sole written authority from God and that it is superior to all other religious books?

11. What would it take for you to place complete confidence in the Bible as truth from God and as the supreme written guide for your life?

With this session you're beginning a journey. Keep in mind that you do not need to feel pressured to "say the right thing" at any point during these discussions. You're taking the time to do this work because you're looking for answers and because you're willing to be honest about your doubts and uncertainties. Others in your group would also benefit from hearing about what you'll be learning. So use these sessions profitably—ask the tough questions, think "outside the box," and learn from what others in your group have to say. But stay authentic about where you are in your journey.

To help you identify your progress more clearly, throughout this guide you will have opportunities to indicate where you are in your spiritual journey. As you gain more spiritual insights, you may find yourself reconsidering your opinions from session to session. The important thing is for you to be completely truthful about what you believe—or don't believe—right now.

12. Pick the statement(s) that best summarizes your view. What reasons do you have for your choice?

_____ The Bible has no relevance for me.
_____ The Bible is an interesting religious book, but it is a mixture of human truth and error.

____ The Bible is no different from other writings that claim to come from God.

____ The Bible has a lot of wisdom, but that doesn't mean it's God's Word.

____ The Bible contains God's truths, yet not everything in it is from God.

____ The Bible—all of it—is God's Word through the words of men.

____ Other: _____

_____

Isn't the Bible Full of Myths?

No One Believes That Anymore!

Much fiction is great literature. The *Iliad* by Homer or the plays of Shakespeare teach us much about human nature and make for wonderful reading. We enjoy their many memorable passages without subjecting them to the rigor of modern historical standards. Their main characters may have some basis in history, but even if the details are erroneous, they stand secure in our cultural treasury as great literary works.

Isn't the same true of the Bible? Its greatness comes from its lofty themes, and the value we get from the narratives is no less if we concede that the events described probably didn't happen. Yet those who want to benefit from the Bible get continually bogged down trying to defend the impossible claim that the stories it contains are factual in every detail. Such assertions make the contemporary believer look silly. God creating the world in six days? A snake who talks in a mythical garden? A boat that contains two of every animal in the world? A sea parting so people can walk through it? Maybe simple people of the past could believe such things, but modern science surely has shown such events to be fictitious.

One reaction to the possibility that the Bible contains myths is to write it off altogether. If the Bible makes untrue statements, it is not worth our time. Leave it in the pile with all the other "fringe" literature—tales

The biblical account of Noah's Ark and the Flood is perhaps the most implausible story for fundamentalists to defend. Where, for example, while loading his ark, did Noah find penguins and polar bears in Palestine?

—Judith Hayes, *In God We Trust: But Which One?*

31

of UFO abductions, writings about worldwide conspiracy theories, ghost stories, and the like. Accept that another of our childhood fantasies unraveled upon further inspection. We got over the others; we can get over this. Move on with life, unfettered by hopes that God shows up and walks on the water.

Another, less severe reaction is to admit that the Bible might make false claims, but let the truth come through in spite of historical errors. Enjoy the stories for what they're worth. Let's not be such literalists; in fact, we'll get more of what the Bible has to offer us if we stay away from such picayune analysis.

Both reactions avoid the embarrassing idea that we have to accept the Bible at face value. Yet there are those who insist these are not the only two viable options. There are a few diehards out there who want us to accept everything the Bible says. They really do believe that when it says God wrote the Ten Commandments in stone, it happened just that way. They take all the miracles of Jesus seriously, including his calming the storm and raising the dead.

Is this unsophisticated approach the one the Bible itself insists we take? Do these literalists have a leg to stand on? Can it possibly be true that the Bible is fact, not fiction?

> The Bible account of the creation of Eve is a preposterous fable.
>
> —Thomas Huxley

OPEN FOR DISCUSSION

1. What is a tall tale or myth you've heard that is popular but not based on history? Why do people enjoy telling these less than truthful stories?

2. What is something in the Bible you think is a myth (or is commonly believed to be a myth)? What aspects of that story seem unreal?

STRAIGHT TALK

Types of Myths

We can speak of three kinds of myths. The first is a story that everyone knows is not real, but that teaches an important lesson. Aesop's fables are a good example of this kind of myth, as are the stories of the Greek and Roman gods.

The second kind of myth is based on a true story that has grown beyond the facts of the original event or person. Stories of King Arthur, Robin Hood, and even men like George Washington and Winston Churchill have fact and fantasy mixed together. These myths are taken more seriously by some, but aspects of these events or persons are questionable.

The third kind of myth is religious dogma. This kind of myth is usually a miraculous event that purports to be real, and many believe wholeheartedly in it. Yet others, who aren't among the faithful, insist there's evidence to the contrary. They contend that faith — not reason — is supporting belief in the myth. Many of the stories in the Bible allegedly fall into this category. Other religions also have their myths, such as Muhammad's ascending to heaven or Krishna's discussions with Arjuna in the Bhagavad Gita. Recent apparitions of the Virgin Mary may also be examples.

3. When people speak of the Bible as being full of myths, to which of the previous types are they referring? What do you think might have motivated a biblical writer who allegedly penned such a myth?

STRAIGHT TALK

History or Fantasy?

Jesus clearly made up most of his parables rather than basing them on real events. Many places in the Bible contain poetic statements such as "the mountains and hills will burst into song before you, and all the trees of the field will clap their hands" (Isaiah 55:12). Author and reader alike know trees don't have hands, but the words describe a real truth poetically.

The controversy comes when events in the Bible are presented as fact but their historicity is questioned. Skepticism arises in two ways. First, a story may be taken literally that the critic claims was intended to be symbolic. In this case the author is exonerated but the gullible readers have made a mistake. Second, a story is presented as fact but the critic contends the writer was simply wrong. In this case the event didn't occur, and some form of pious fraud or self-delusion is at work — both writer and believing readers have erred.

The following are some of the alleged myths of the Bible.

- the creation story
- Noah and the ark
- the ten plagues of Egypt
- the parting of the Red Sea
- the walls of Jericho falling
- the sun standing still
- Jonah and the whale

4. What clues would you look for in trying to determine if a story in the Bible was meant to be taken at face value?

5. Do you think believers generally investigate the biblical stories they read to determine whether they have a basis in fact? Why do you think some people are so ready to accept everything they read in the Bible without questioning it?

The day will come, when the mystical generation of Jesus, by the Supreme Being as His Father, in the womb of a virgin, will be classed with the fable of the generation of Minerva in the brain of Jupiter.

—Thomas Jefferson

6. Do you believe that critics of the Bible's miraculous stories have solid evidence that contradicts the Bible's claims? What other possible motives or reasons might lay behind a skeptical stance?

Flood Stories

Myths about a great flood exist in many cultures. One famous Babylonian story, *The Gilgamesh Epic,* tells of a man who built a big ship to ride out a flood. His boat was a huge cube, however, which would slowly roll in the water. By contrast, the proportions of Noah's ark (approximately 450 feet long, 75 feet wide, 45 feet high) are those of a stable, seaworthy vessel.

7. How does the presence of other flood stories affect the probability of a historical event giving rise to them all?

8. In his teachings, Jesus referred to many of the so-called mythical parts of the Bible—the creation stories, Moses at the burning bush, Noah and the ark, and Jonah and the great fish, to name a few—and he never seemed to doubt their truth. Jesus challenged his listeners in many other areas where he believed they misunderstood the Old Testament, but he said nothing to attempt to revise their understanding of its history. Do you think it is reasonable to accept the historical accuracy of the more difficult parts of the Bible when the witness of Jesus and other verifiable claims show its overall trustworthiness? Why or why not?

I have read, in Greek and Latin, scores of myths but I did not find the slightest flavor of myth here [in the Gospels]. Most people who know their Greek and Latin, whatever their attitude to the New Testament narratives, would agree.

—J. B. Phillips

HEART OF THE MATTER

9. Why is it sometimes hard to accept stories that contain supernatural elements?

10. What kind of research could a person do to help him or her gain more confidence in the stories told in the Bible?

11. On a scale from one to ten, place an X near the spot and phrase that best describes you. What reasons do you have for placing your X where you did?

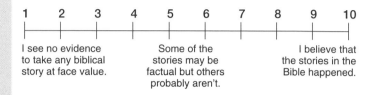

1 2 3 4 5 6 7 8 9 10

I see no evidence to take any biblical story at face value.

Some of the stories may be factual but others probably aren't.

I believe that the stories in the Bible happened.

What About All Those Contradictions?

What's the Truth?

The politician smiles the million-dollar smile that got him elected. With his smooth, calming voice, he assures his constituency that his programs are working, the future is bright, and if we just stick with him, all will be well.

But the newspapers tell another story. There's corruption among the politician's administration. The statistics he so eloquently quotes can be interpreted in a very different way, reflecting poorly on his policies. Someone close to the man has accused him of illegal activities, and others tell stories of improper moral conduct.

Two portraits, one person. Which is reality?

We can know the truth only if we test the facts. We can know if a person is lying only if we examine his claims and compare what he says with what can be verified. If we find that what we know to be true is contradicting the truth we're being asked to accept, it's reasonable to reject the messenger—smile and all.

There may be times when direct validation of a particular statement is impossible. In those cases we have to go with what seems most likely in light of the facts we do know, and the reliability of the one making the claim. The trustworthiness of any person must be established before we commit our well-being into his hands. For example, there will be times when we

> According to the Bible, God was ignorant, a ruthless liar and cheat; he broke his pledges, changed his mind so often that he grew weary of repenting. He was a murderer of children, ordered his people to slay, rape, steal, and lie and commit every foul and filthy abomination in human power. In fact, the more I read the Bible the less I find in it that is either credible or admirable.
>
> —Rupert Hughes

During many ages there were witches. The Bible said so. The Bible commanded that they should not be allowed to live. Therefore the Church, after doing its duty in but a lazy and indolent way for 800 years, gathered up its halters, thumbscrews, and firebrands, and set about its holy work in earnest. She worked hard at it night and day during nine centuries and imprisoned, tortured, hanged, and burned whole hordes and armies of witches, and washed the Christian world clean with their foul blood. Then it was discovered that there was no such thing as witches, and never had been. One does not know whether to laugh or to cry.

—Mark Twain

will put our trust in an elected official, and our trust will be warranted—and rewarded. There are other times when we will trust in the wrong person and be disappointed.

Certainly, in the case of the Bible, where our eternal well-being is at stake, there must be validation of the measurable (history, science, archaeology) for us to trust the immeasurable (spiritual truths, heavenly realities, unquantifiable claims). If the Bible holds up under our scrutiny, we can reasonably rely on it for things we cannot directly validate. If there are significant contradictions, it tells us that the writers are not concerned with truth.

Contradictions would prove that the Bible is speaking not with one voice but with many voices—some of which are manifestly wrong. And if the Bible has no unified voice, it is not what it claims to be: the reliable and trustworthy words of an utterly truthful God.

OPEN FOR DISCUSSION

1. Can you recall a time when you saw or heard something disturbing about someone you trusted? What was it like to feel mistrust for someone who had been worthy of trust up to that point?

2. People often say, "There are so many contradictions in the Bible," yet often can't name one they've found for themselves. Have you read anything in the Bible that you believe is a true contradiction? Explain. What has this done to your level of confidence in the Bible?

3. One common contradiction people suggest is the way the two testaments portray God. The Old Testament, they say, shows God as harsh, judgmental, and quick to punish wrongdoing. The New Testament God is a much more likable guy: loving, patient, and anxious to forgive. Do you think this issue of how God is portrayed constitutes a contradiction? Why or why not?

> There is not the slightest question but that the God of the Old Testament is a jealous, vengeful God, inflicting not only on the sinful "pagans" but even on his Chosen People fire, lightning, hideous plagues and diseases, brimstone, and other curses.
>
> —Steve Allen

STRAIGHT TALK
Contradictions and the Character of God

Clearly, the God of the Bible is a multidimensional being, brimming with compassion as well as grief over sin and its consequences. The confusion for many of us is not that the Old and New Testaments paint different pictures of God but that we have a hard time comprehending how a loving God can also be holy and righteous. This probably stems from our lack of human models: the gentle people we know aren't easily ruffled, and the people we know who got angry do so destructively.

In Jesus of course we see a splendid example of both tenderness and righteous indignation. Here is someone so compassionate that he gently holds and prays for little children and touches the sick and dying. Yet he also rails at the religious leaders for their stubborn refusal to put God above their traditions, and overturns the tables of the greedy money changers who've obstructed worship. In Jesus we see all that God is: holiness, tenderness, forgiveness, and righteousness. The gospel of John put it even more clearly: "Grace and truth came through Jesus Christ. No one has ever seen God, but God the One and Only, who is at the Father's side, has made him known" (John 1:17–18).

4. To what extent does your view of God incorporate the different aspects (listed above) of who God is? How might your view of him need to be revised?

STRAIGHT TALK

Contradictions and the Cross

Some people point to the inscription on the cross of Jesus as an example of how the Gospels contradict themselves. Each gospel records the words differently.

> THIS IS JESUS, THE KING OF THE JEWS (Matthew 27:37).
> THE KING OF THE JEWS (Mark 15:26).
> THIS IS THE KING OF THE JEWS (Luke 23:38).
> JESUS OF NAZARETH, THE KING OF THE JEWS (John 19:19).

5. Do you think these inscriptions constitute a contradiction? Why or why not?

6. What additional light is added by the detail from John 19:20, which states, "Many of the Jews read this sign, for the place where Jesus was crucified was near the city, and the sign was written in Aramaic, Latin and Greek"?

7. Does the slight variation in this wording offer any positive evidence that the gospel writers are reliable historians? Explain. What do the differences in wording suggest about the integrity of the early copyists who let the differences remain in the manuscripts?

STRAIGHT TALK

Contradictions and the Resurrection of Jesus

Another alleged contradiction is the differing accounts of the disciples' visits to the tomb of Jesus and of his resurrection appearances. These accounts can be found in Matthew 28:1–15; Mark 16:1–14; Luke 24:1–49; and John 20:1–31. Here are some of the questions that might be raised.

> Was there one angel at the tomb or two?
> How many women went to the tomb — was Mary alone or with others?
> Were the angels outside or inside the tomb?
> Who actually went into the tomb?
> Did Peter go into the tomb or just look in?

Do these differences constitute true contradictions?

Consider the following story. A woman was waiting for a bus with a friend. As the bus approached, the crowd pressed forward and she was pushed in the path of the bus. The bus struck her and an ambulance was called. Meanwhile, the friend called the woman's husband and told him, "Your wife has been hit by a bus. I'll call you when we find out what hospital she's been taken to." About an hour later, the husband received another call. This time it was a police officer. "I'm sorry to inform you, Sir, but your wife has just been killed in a car accident." When the man expressed his shock that he had heard her injuries from being hit by the bus were not that severe, the officer replied that there was no bus involved and that she had been killed while a passenger in an automobile.

From the looks of the above story, the police officer and the friend are contradicting each other. Somebody is mistaken about what vehicles were involved and the nature of the woman's injuries (or else one or both of those people called the wrong husband!). In any event, if we were reading this account in two different newspapers (one story from the officer and one story from the friend), it is hard not to assume the accounts are mixed up. If you read those stories, you'd want to ask some more questions to find out what really went on.

As it turns out, both the friend and the police officer were one hundred percent correct in every detail. The woman had been hit by a bus. Before the ambulance arrived, a passerby offered to take her to the hospital. While en route in that car, the woman was involved in the fatal auto accident. The two stories can be completely harmonized, omitting nothing. Had someone tampered with either story to erase the contradiction, the final story would not have been true to the actual events. So leaving the stories as they are, even with apparent contradictions, is a more honest and credible option. That is how the Gospels come to us. In many cases they can be made to complement each other without negating each other.

— Quoted in *Follow Me!* from the
Walking with God small group series

HEART OF THE MATTER

8. If God is behind the Bible, why do you think he hasn't eliminated all possible areas of confusion?

9. Other than a desire to seek truth, what might motivate someone to look for contradictions in the Bible? What does it tell you about a person when he or she seems to delight in trying to ridicule the Bible?

STRAIGHT TALK
Assessing a Seeming Contradiction

When we read something that looks like a contradiction, it may be helpful to ask the following questions.

Do I understand what I've read — could I have misinterpreted something?

Is there simply an omission of fact rather than a true contradiction here?

Is the writer speaking in general terms (summarizing) rather than giving specific data?

Can other knowledgeable people who've studied the Bible contribute to my understanding?

Is it likely that I'm the first one in history who's encountered an unresolvable issue here?

Are there reasons for trusting the Bible's general reliability even if I have to hold this issue as an open question for now?

10. How might the above rules help you to handle problems that arise when you're reading the Bible?

11. Pick the statement(s) that best summarizes your view. What reasons do you have for your choice?

_____ The Bible has clearly contradictory statements that cause me to question its credibility.

_____ The Bible has contradictions, but I need to know more before I completely reject it.

_____ The Bible has apparent contradictions that I am trying to understand.

_____ I believe the Bible even if it has contradictions.

_____ The Bible may have contradictions, but I'm sure more evidence will bear out its truthfulness.

_____ God still speaks through the Bible in spite of its contradictions.

_____ Other: _____

_____

Hasn't the Bible Changed Over Time?

A Garbled Transmission?

Remember playing "telephone"? You whisper some brief message to a friend—for example, "The boy in the photograph was eating something from the ice-cream store. When he turned around, his family surprised him with a new bicycle." The same story is whispered by your friend to another person, and then that person tells another. The story goes around the whole room, and then the last person reports what she heard. The result? "The photographer bought a tricycle for everyone who worked at the Dairy Queen!" What happened to the original story? It got changed—lost—in transmission.

Isn't it reasonable to assume that the same thing happened with the Bible? There were no tape recorders running when Jesus spoke. Even if someone took notes as he gave his messages (and there's absolutely no evidence that anybody did), how accurate could the resulting reconstruction be? From what we know, the stories of Jesus weren't written down until decades later. Wouldn't there be substantial loss of detail? None of the things we take for granted today that make accuracy possible—photocopiers, computers, fax machines, digitized recordings—were available back then.

> Citing the Bible as evidence for anything is like saying that the sun is in fact a chariot of fire that races across the sky because we read about it in Greek mythology.
>
> —Stephen Ban

Now back up even centuries earlier. At the time when Moses spoke to a nation of former slaves, there was even less of a probability of having what he said be accurately recorded. Could a preliterate culture, in which only kings and nobility had the tools of reading and writing, faithfully preserve centuries of history, and proclamations supposedly from God? It stretches the limits of credulity to believe so.

Let's suppose, for the sake of argument, that some of the facts got through uncorrupted. In spite of all odds, let's agree that some truth—maybe even lots of truth—is accurately preserved in the Bible. Which parts have that truth? How can we possibly know, out of a single chapter of the Bible, if the first paragraph is accurate and the others are in error, or whether the first paragraph is wrong but the rest are okay? As long as we have no way of knowing which parts of the Bible are truthful and which parts aren't, it doesn't matter that some truth resides there—we can never get to it with certainty. If a man is a careful scholar but has an odd habit of telling one lie a day, we can never trust anything he says, because we never know which statement is his allotted daily lie. Truth mixed with untruth in the Bible gets us nowhere. We may as well have no truth at all.

For those who believe the Bible to be trustworthy, these are tough questions that need answers. In this session we will suggest four reasons why the Bible can be trusted to be an accurate historical record, uncorrupted by centuries of transmission (copying): (1) unparalleled manuscript support (quantity and quality), (2) careful copying techniques, (3) validation from secular sources, and (4) validation from archaeology.

In the early parts of the Bible's story, biblical persons have yet to be identified correctly in any external sources. There have been many attempts, and some confident claims, but as yet there is no good reason to identify Moses or Joseph with any known person or period in ancient Egyptian records.

—Robin Lane Fox,
The Unauthorized Version

1. Do you remember a funny story about a time when you gave someone important instructions and they misunderstood you (or vice versa)? Describe what happened.

2. It is often noted that the Bible has been translated into many languages and that therefore the Bible you have before you may be a translation of a translation of a translation. Does knowing that the Bible has been translated so many times cause you to lose confidence in the accuracy of the Bible you read now? Why or why not?

STRAIGHT TALK

Translation vs. Transmission

People sometimes confuse the effects of translation (creating a new document in a new language) with the effects of transmission (copying a document word-for-word to make a second, identical document). An ancient document can be translated into a thousand different languages, and as long as we keep going back to the oldest manuscripts for each new translation, the number of translations has no bearing on the accuracy of the version before us. Virtually every English Bible around today has been translated from ancient Greek and Hebrew manuscripts. Scholars who make a modern translation do not use more recent versions and certainly don't go to other translations (for example, a French Bible) as a source; instead they start with the oldest and most reliable manuscripts of the Old and New Testament and then make their translation fresh from those primary sources (which are very close to the original writings).

3. Even if the Bible in your hand was made from ancient copies (not recent ones, and not other translations), do you think it's a problem that no original of any book of the Bible exists from which to make translations? Why or why not?

Unparalleled Manuscript Support

Author	When Written	Earliest Copy	Time Span	Number of Copies
Caesar	100–44 B.C.	A.D. 900	1,000 years	10
Tacitus	A.D. 100	A.D. 1100	1,000 years	20
Suetonius	A.D. 75–160	A.D. 950	800 years	8
Herodotus	480–425 B.C.	A.D. 900	1,300 years	8
Aristotle	384–322 B.C.	A.D. 1100	1,400 years	49
New Testament	A.D. 45–100	fragment: A.D. 125; full copies: third and fourth centuries	fragment: 25 years; full copies: 200–300 years	24,000

compiled from Josh McDowell, *Evidence That Demands a Verdict*

4. In view of the above table, what is your reaction to the number of New Testament manuscripts in comparison with the number of other works of ancient history?

It seems strange that the text of Shakespeare, which has been in existence less than two hundred and eight years, should be far more uncertain and corrupt than that of the New Testament, now over eighteen centuries old.... With perhaps a dozen or twenty exceptions, the text of every verse in the New Testament may be said to be ... settled by general consent.... But in every one of Shakespeare's thirty-seven plays there are probably a hundred readings still in dispute.

—John Lea, *The Greatest Book in the World*

5. On top of all the New Testament manuscript evidence, there are many ancient writers who quoted extensively from the Bible (even as authors do today). Those ancient sermons, letters, and other writings include so many New Testament citations that even if we were to lose every copy we have of the Bible—including all those ancient manuscripts—scholars could reconstruct the entire New Testament with the exception of eleven verses! What do you think is the value of having all these citations from the New Testament in nonbiblical sources?

STRAIGHT TALK

Careful Copying Techniques

The scribes who copied the Bible were trained professionals with stringent job performance standards. For example, rules for the Talmudists (A.D. 100–500) included:

> No word or letter must be written from memory without the scribe looking at the codex before him.
>
> Between every consonant the width of a hair or thread must intervene.
>
> Between every section (parashah), the breadth of nine consonants.
>
> Between every book, three lines.
>
> The fifth book of Moses must terminate exactly with a line, but the rest need not do so.
>
> The copyist must sit in full Jewish dress and be recently bathed.

He should not begin to write the name of God with a pen newly dipped in ink.

If a king addresses him while writing the divine name, the scribe should ignore him.

The Massoretes who followed (A.D. 500–900) likewise exercised great care in copying. As Sir Frederick Kenyon noted in *Our Bible and the Ancient Manuscripts,*

> They numbered the verses, words, and letters of every book. They calculated the middle word and the middle letter of each. They enumerated verses which contained all the letters of the alphabet, or a certain number of them; and so on. These trivialities, as we may rightly consider them, had yet the effect of securing minute attention to the precise transmission of the text; and they are but an excessive manifestation of a respect for the sacred scriptures which in itself deserves nothing but praise. The Massoretes were indeed anxious that not one jot nor tittle, not one smallest letter nor one tiny part of a letter, of the Law should pass away or be lost.

6. How do these rules for accurate transmission affect your overall trust in the text of the Bible?

STRAIGHT TALK

Validation from Secular Sources

Often nonbiblical sources describe events recorded in the Bible. The following are a few examples.

> Now some of the Jews thought that Herod's army had been destroyed by God, and that it was a very just penalty to avenge John, surnamed the Baptist. For Herod had killed him,

though he was a good man, who bade the Jews practise virtue, be just one to another and pious toward God, and come together in baptism.

—Flavius Josephus, Antiquities XVIII.5.2,
writing around A.D. 100

Hence to suppress the rumor, he falsely charged with the guilt, and punished with the most exquisite tortures, the persons commonly called Christians, who were hated for their enormities. Christus, the founder of the name, was put to death by Pontius Pilate, procurator of Judea in the reign of Tiberius: but the pernicious superstition, repressed for a time broke out again, not only through Judea, where the mischief originated, but through the city of Rome also.

—Tacitus, Annals XV.44, writing around A.D. 100

They affirmed, however, that the whole of their guilt, or their error, was, that they were in the habit of meeting on a certain fixed day before it was light, when they sang in alternate verse a hymn to Christ as to a god, and bound themselves to a solemn oath, not to any wicked deeds, but never to commit any fraud, theft, adultery, never to falsify their word, not to deny a trust when they should be called upon to deliver it up.

—Pliny, governor of Bithynia, Epistles X.96,
writing to the emperor Trajan, explaining
what the Christians he arrested said to him

---

7. Does nonbiblical support for biblical events make any difference to you when you read the Bible? Why or why not?

STRAIGHT TALK

Validation from Archaeology

Since 1974 seventeen thousand tablets have been unearthed from ancient Ebla (now northern Syria). These writings corroborate the world of the patriarchs (around 2000 B.C.). In his book *Evidence That Demands a Verdict,* Josh McDowell states,

> The victory of Abraham over Chedolaomer and the Mesopotamian kings has been described as fictitious and the five Cities of the Plain (Sodom, Gomorrah, Adamah, Zeboiim, and Zoar) as legendary. Yet the Ebla archives refer to all five Cities of the Plain and on one tablet the cities are listed in the exact same sequence as Genesis 14. The milieu of the tablets reflect the culture of the patriarchal period and depict that, before the catastrophe recorded in Genesis 14, the area was a flourishing region experiencing prosperity and success, as recorded in Genesis.

In 1961 a tablet was found during a renovation of the amphitheater in Caesarea (on the Mediterranean Sea). This tablet had the name Pontius Pilate inscribed on it. Until that time, the name Pilate was found only in the New Testament and in a few other secular historical sources. This find is just one more validation that the people and events of the Bible are real.

8. What bearing do these kinds of archaeological discoveries have on your trust in the Bible?

9. What is the cumulative effect for you of all this evidence for the reliability of the Bible?

10. Do you think if someone was intent on being skeptical, any amount of evidence would persuade them? Do you think any error would convince someone committed to believing the Bible that there are reasons not to trust it? Explain your answers.

CHARTING YOUR JOURNEY

11. On a scale from one to ten, place an X near the spot and phrase that best describes you. What reasons do you have for placing your X where you did?

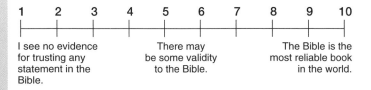

1 2 3 4	5 6 7	8 9 10
I see no evidence for trusting any statement in the Bible.	There may be some validity to the Bible.	The Bible is the most reliable book in the world.

Why Should I Trust the Bible?

A Biased Record?

We've all seen how Madison Avenue can make any product seem to be the very thing we need to make our lives complete. When a company is intent on selling its product, they'll stop at almost nothing to make that product seem irresistible. Facts or no facts, the ad makes it clear this is what we really need, at any price.

Hasn't Christianity done the same thing with the Bible? Here is the book that supposedly tells what God has said over the years, and most important, tells us everything we need to know about Jesus. But the Bible was put out by those who wanted to "sell" Jesus. How can we be sure they haven't glossed over important information that might reflect less favorably on their leader?

We've all seen the smiling faces of freshly scrubbed followers who've joined some cult group. The cult members seem so sincere, yet when we hear their leader talk, it's obvious he is a fraud. Why are we able to perceive that this man's claims are bogus, but his gullible followers cannot? Once again, isn't it a case of those who are "in" seeing what they want to see and not seeing what they don't want to see? Why wouldn't the same thing happen to those early followers of Jesus?

When examining the claims of the Bible, we must allow for the possibility of this kind of bias. We must

> If 50 million people believe a foolish thing, it is still a foolish thing.
>
> —Anatole France

also ask what features of the Bible make it stand out as truthful—more so than other books which claim to be divine revelation. We need to know we're getting not just the approved party line but accurate information. We need to find out whether the Bible has something to commend it other than a lot of people thinking it's special. (After all, truth isn't subject to a majority vote!) We need to discover whether these writers were just blowing smoke or if in fact God seemed to be present somehow in what they wrote.

In this session we will suggest three more reasons why we can trust the Bible's message: (1) credible authors who cared about accuracy, (2) prophecy that shows supernatural involvement, and (3) transformative teachings.

OPEN FOR DISCUSSION

1. What "heirloom story" have you heard about something a member of your family did in generations past? Do you consider this story truthful even though you weren't there? Why or why not?

2. How does knowing that Jesus never wrote down a word of his teaching affect you as you read the Gospels? If you have confidence in what you're reading, what is the basis for that trust?

Credible Authors Who Cared About Accuracy

Luke begins his gospel with these words:

> Many have undertaken to draw up an account of the things that have been fulfilled among us, just as they were handed down to us by those who from the first were eyewitnesses and servants of the word. Therefore, since I myself have carefully investigated everything from the beginning, it seemed good also to me to write an orderly account for you, most excellent Theophilus, so that you may know the certainty of the things you have been taught.
>
> — Luke 1:1–4

Sir William Ramsay, considered one of the world's greatest archaeologists, was at one time skeptical about a first-century date for Luke and Acts. He eventually conceded after extensive research, "Luke is a historian of the first rank; not merely are his statements of fact trustworthy . . . this author should be placed along with the very greatest of historians." He added, "Luke's history is unsurpassed in respect of its trustworthiness."

3. Why is it important to know that writers like Luke did research and that their historical statements stand up to later authentication?

Few intelligent Christians can still hold to the idea that the Bible is an infallible Book, that it contains no linguistic errors, no historical discrepancies, no antiquated scientific assumptions, not even bad ethical standards. Historical investigation and literary criticism have taken the magic out of the Bible and have made it a composite human book, written by many hands in different ages. The existence of thousands of variations of texts makes it impossible to hold the doctrine of a book verbally infallible. Some might claim for the original copies of the Bible an infallible character, but this view only begs the question and makes such Christian apologetics more ridiculous in the eyes of the sincere man.

—Elmer Homrighausen, former dean of Princeton Theological Seminary

4. The assumption has been made that without modern methods of writing and copying, we can't know with any degree of certainty what Jesus actually said. Comment on this assumption in light of the following facts.

1. Many first-century Jewish rabbis had their disciples commit their teachings to memory; Jesus, as a rabbi, probably did the same.

2. In a culture in which people are not accustomed to writing things down, their minds recall details without written aids; people keep accurate records mentally because they have to.

3. The disciples heard Jesus give the same messages over and over as they traveled to different cities; this would have the effect of engraving the teachings in their memories.

4. Many of Jesus' teachings are stories and parables, which are by nature easier to remember than information that is more technical.

5. The disciples had many vivid experiences with Jesus, which would have left lasting impressions, more so than would casual, inconsequential events.

6. With lots of people hearing Jesus' messages, later historians (like Luke) could interview these people and write accounts that take all the various recollections and combine them in a composite document.

7. The Gospels were written within the lifetime of Jesus' contemporaries; those who knew the facts to be otherwise could have easily stepped forward to contradict the claims contained in them. Also, the book of Acts alludes to Jesus' enemies knowing about his claims and the Resurrection without ever questioning these historical facts (Acts 2:22; 26:26).

5. The writers below express that they were eyewitnesses of the events they recorded. Why is this important in documents meant to bring readers to faith?

We did not follow cleverly invented stories when we told you about the power and coming of our Lord Jesus Christ, but we were eyewitnesses of his majesty. For he received honor and glory from God the Father when the voice came to him from the Majestic Glory, saying, "This is my Son, whom I love; with him I am well pleased." We ourselves heard this voice that came from heaven when we were with him on the sacred mountain.

—2 Peter 1:16–18

That which was from the beginning, which we have heard, which we have seen with our eyes, which we have looked at and our hands have touched—this we proclaim concerning the Word of life. The life appeared; we have seen it and testify to it, and we proclaim to you the eternal life, which was with the Father and has appeared to us. We proclaim to you what we have seen and heard, so that you also may have fellowship with us.

—1 John 1:1–3

The man who saw it has given testimony, and his testimony is true. He knows that he tells the truth, and he testifies so that you also may believe.

—John 19:35

What I received I passed on to you as of first importance: that Christ died for our sins according to the Scriptures, that he was buried, that he was raised on the third day according to the Scriptures, and that he appeared to Peter, and then to the Twelve. After that, he appeared to more than five hundred of the brothers at the same time, most of whom are still living, though some have fallen asleep. Then he appeared to James, then to all the apostles, and last of all he appeared to me also, as to one abnormally born.

—1 Corinthians 15:3–8

6. Some people argue that because the gospel writers were followers of Jesus, they were biased and distorted historical information to agree with their bias. What is your reaction to this argument?

STRAIGHT TALK

Prophecy That Shows Supernatural Involvement

Think of how many religions attempt to validate themselves with prophecy. Think of how many people rely on these prophecies, however vague, however unfulfilled, to support or prop up their beliefs. Yet has there ever been a religion with the prophetic accuracy and reliability of science?

— Carl Sagan, *The Demon-Haunted World: Science As a Candle in the Dark*

It is the only volume ever produced by man, or a group of men, in which is to be found a large body of prophecies relating to individual nations, to Israel, to all the peoples of the earth, to certain cities, and to the coming of One who was to be the Messiah. The ancient world had many different devices for determining the future, known as divination, but not in the entire gamut of Greek and Latin literature, even though they use the words prophet and prophecy, can we find any real specific prophecy of a great historic event to come in the distant future, nor any prophecy of a Savior to arise in the human race. . . .

[Islam] cannot point to any prophecies of the coming of Mohammed uttered hundreds of years before his birth. Neither can the founders of any cult in this country rightly identify any ancient text specifically foretelling their appearance.

— Wilbur Smith, *The Incomparable Book*

7. From the above quotes, are you inclined to agree more with the reasoning of Carl Sagan or Wilbur Smith? Why?

8. Jesus' birthplace in Bethlehem (Micah 5:2), his Galilean heritage (Isaiah 9:1–7), and the peculiar circumstances surrounding his burial (Isaiah 53:9) are among many prophecies that foretell his coming. According to Peter Stoner in *Science Speaks,* the probabilities that any one person fulfilled merely eight of the numerous prophecies predicting the Messiah are 1 in 10^{17} (100,000,000,000,000,000). Other than supernatural involvement, what do you think could explain Jesus' fulfillment of messianic prophecies from the Bible?

STRAIGHT TALK

Transformative Teaching

The Bible has remarkable power to transform lives. In his book *Knowing Scripture,* R. C. Sproul states, "You want me to make the Bible come alive? I didn't know that it had died! In fact, I never even heard that it was ill. . . . No, I can't make the Bible come alive for anyone. The Bible is already alive. It made me come alive."

9. Many people will testify to the life-changing message they encounter in the Bible. What are both the strengths and weaknesses of this way of validating the trustworthiness of the Bible?

HEART OF THE MATTER

10. Between the last session and this one, what piece of evidence about the trustworthiness of the Bible has been most helpful to you?

11. What aspects of the Bible's message are you more willing to consider since this study began?

12. On a scale from one to ten, place an X near the spot and phrase that best describes you. What reasons do you have for placing your X where you did?

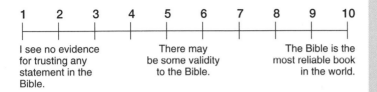

| 1 | 2 | 3 | 4 | 5 | 6 | 7 | 8 | 9 | 10 |

I see no evidence for trusting any statement in the Bible.

There may be some validity to the Bible.

The Bible is the most reliable book in the world.

Is the Bible Really God's Book?

This Is Divine?

Have you ever compiled an unbiased list of what kinds of stories are in the Bible? Among the more bizarre tales, you'll find wars advocated by God himself—death and destruction by divine decree. Men and women are enslaved, children are killed without mercy. Some of the heroes of the Bible are crooks and cheats, and often the "good guys" finish last—or not at all. God sometimes appears upset over trivialities, and at other times seemingly overlooks huge moral defects. Both he and his people are a fickle bunch. Yet we are expected to believe that these stories constitute God's written revelation to humankind, forming the basis for civilized action in the world today.

The Bible also contains detailed descriptions of a ritual system responsible for the slaughter of thousands if not millions of animals. Does the Almighty really want all this bloodshed? What possible pleasure could God get from watching some poor helpless animal die? Isn't it bad enough that people do evil deeds—does the added evil of an animal dying somehow make up for it? How could such a system be created, enscripturated, and perpetrated by the supposed loving Creator of the universe?

Then there are all the silly things in the Bible. Why does the Bible contain all those genealogies? Who cares who "begat" whom? Why is so much of the

One does well to put on gloves when reading the New Testament. The proximity of so much uncleanliness almost forces one to do this.

—Friedrich Nietzsche

Bible dedicated to obscure history—to the exploits of a fairly small minority in the ancient world? What does that have to do with God telling all people at all times how to live? Why does the cosmology of the Bible sound so unscientific when it's supposed to come from Someone who knows that the earth goes around the sun, that the stars are not holes poked out of a hard shell above us, and that if heaven is "up" in Palestine, heaven would be "down" in South America. No matter where you open it, the Bible sounds so human—full of estimates and guesses (based on limited knowledge), quaint observations, and clearly reflecting the viewpoints of those who wrote it rather than the error-free perspective of an all-knowing God.

Maybe we could grant that the Bible is a well-loved book and for some inexplicable reason has become immensely popular. But it is a huge jump in logic from that premise to the conclusion that this book comes from God and should be regarded as the sole authority for accurate religious knowledge. What possible compelling arguments can anyone offer to suggest we overlook its flaws and human side and grant it divine status?

OPEN FOR DISCUSSION

1. From what you've observed, what unhealthy attitudes and practices can be adopted by people who believe that the Bible is God's Word? What positive changes have you seen?

2. What evidence would someone need in order to gain confidence that any writings (including the Koran, the Book of Mormon, Science and Health, or other so-called revelations from God) are not just extraordinary but God's words?

3. Was there ever a time when you decided to find out once and for all if any writings (which may or may not have included the Bible) were really from God? If so, what did you discover in your search? If not, what would it take for you to embark on such an investigation?

4. One piece of evidence people give in support of the Bible being divinely inspired is fulfilled prophecy. Do you believe this is sufficient to establish the Bible as God's book? Why or why not?

5. Another reason people give as proof that the Bible is from God is the beneficial effects it has for those who believe its message. What are the strengths and weaknesses of such an argument?

STRAIGHT TALK

An Argument for the Divine Inspiration of the Bible

1. The Gospels are reasonably accurate ancient records (not necessarily without error and not necessarily from God), which record many facts concerning Jesus, his life, and his teachings.

2. These ancient documents accurately record Jesus as saying in several different places that the Bible (the Old Testament of his day) was God's Word down to a "jot and tittle" (Matthew 5:17–19; 15:3–9; 22:29, 31–32; Luke 4:16–21; 24:25–27, 44–45; John 5:46–47; 10:35).

3. The Gospels also accurately recount Jesus saying there would be a coming record of his teaching to be prepared by his disciples with the help of the Holy Spirit and their own memories.

4. Jesus performed miracles and even rose from the dead, thus validating all his claims about himself and any other teaching he gave.

5. Because of Jesus' credentials (most significantly the Resurrection), anything he says must be true; God would not resurrect a liar or self-deceived person and thereby give credence to something that wasn't fact.

Therefore, because Jesus taught the divine inspiration of the Scriptures, we have compelling reason to also believe, as he did, in their divine authorship and utter reliability.

6. Which of the above premises are strongest and which are weak, in your opinion?

7. Does the argument convince you? Why or why not?

8. What other reasons have you heard or would you give for asserting that the Bible is God's Word?

9. Do you believe it is enough to "just pray about it" to know if the Bible is from God? Why or why not?

It ain't the parts of the Bible that I can't understand that bother me, it is the parts that I do understand.

—Mark Twain

10. What factors other than lack of evidence might contribute to your (or someone else's) hesitancy in accepting the Bible? What factors other than rational arguments might contribute to your (or someone else's) acceptance of the Bible?

11. What difference would it make in your every-day experience to believe that the Bible is God's Word?

12. Pick the statement(s) that best summarizes your view. What reasons do you have for your choice?

_____ The Bible is, pure and simple, a human book.

_____ The Bible is a mixture of human truth and error.

_____ The Bible has remarkable wisdom, but it did not come from God.

_____ The Bible has a lot of value and God works through it, but that doesn't mean it's the only book God uses.

_____ The Bible contains God's truths, yet not everything in it is from God.

_____ Other books, not just the Bible, have been inspired by God.

_____ The Bible—all of it and only it—is God's Word through the words of men.

_____ Other: _____

_____

Recommended Resources

Ken Boa and Larry Moody, *I'm Glad You Asked* (Chariot Victor, 1995).

Gregory Boyd and Edward Boyd, *Letters from a Skeptic* (Chariot Victor, 1994).

William Lane Craig, *Reasonable Faith* (Crossway, 1994).

C. Stephen Evans, *Why Believe?* (Eerdmans, 1996).

Cliffe Knechtle, *Give Me an Answer* (InterVarsity, 1986).

Andrew Knowles, *Finding Faith* (Lion, 1994).

Peter Kreeft and Ronald Tacelli, *Handbook of Christian Apologetics* (InterVarsity, 1994).

C. S. Lewis, *Mere Christianity* (HarperSanFransisco, 2001).

C. S. Lewis, *Miracles* (HarperSanFransisco, 2001).

Paul Little, *Know What You Believe* (Chariot Victor, 1987).

Paul Little, *Know Why You Believe* (InterVarsity, 2000).

J. P. Moreland, *Scaling the Secular City,* (Baker, 1987).

R. C. Sproul, *Reason to Believe,* (Zondervan, 1982).

Lee Strobel, *The Case for Christ* (Zondervan, 1998).

Lee Strobel, *The Case for Faith* (Zondervan, 2000).

Willow Creek Association
Vision, Training, Resources for Prevailing Churches

This resource was created to serve you and to help you in building a local church that prevails!

Since 1992, the Willow Creek Association (WCA) has been linking like-minded, action-oriented churches with each other and with strategic vision, training, and resources. Now a worldwide network of over 6,400 churches from more than ninety denominations, the WCA works to equip Member Churches and others with the tools needed to build prevailing churches. Our desire is to inspire, equip, and encourage Christian leaders to build biblically functioning churches that reach increasing numbers of unchurched people, not just with innovations from Willow Creek Community Church in South Barrington, Illinois, but from any church in the world that has experienced God-given breakthroughs.

WILLOW CREEK CONFERENCES

Each year, thousands of local church leaders, staff and volunteers—from WCA Member Churches and others—attend one of our conferences or training events. Conferences offered on the Willow Creek campus in South Barrington, Illinois, include:

Prevailing Church Conference: Foundational training for staff and volunteers working to build a prevailing local church.

Prevailing Church Workshops: More than fifty strategic, day-long workshops covering seven topic areas that represent key characteristics of a prevailing church; offered twice each year.

Promiseland Conference: Children's ministries; infant through fifth grade.

Student Ministries Conference: Junior and senior high ministries.

Willow Creek Arts Conference: Vision and training for Christian artists using their gifts in the ministries of local churches.

Leadership Summit: Envisioning and equipping Christians with leadership gifts and responsibilities; broadcast live via satellite to eighteen cities across North America.

Contagious Evangelism Conference: Encouragement and training for churches and church leaders who want to be strategic in reaching lost people for Christ.

Small Groups Conference: Exploring how developing a church *of* small groups can play a vital role in developing authentic Christian community that leads to spiritual transformation.

To find out more about WCA conferences, visit our website at www.willowcreek.com.

PREVAILING CHURCH REGIONAL WORKSHOPS

Each year the WCA team leads several, two-day training events in select cities across the United States. Some twenty day-long workshops are offered in topic areas including leadership, next-generation ministries, small groups, arts and worship, evangelism, spiritual gifts, financial stewardship, and spiritual formation. These events make quality training more accessible and affordable to larger groups of staff and volunteers.

To find out more about Prevailing Church Regional Workshops, visit our website at www.willowcreek.com.

WILLOW CREEK RESOURCES™

Churches can look to Willow Creek Resources™ for a trusted channel of ministry tools in areas of leadership, evangelism, spiritual gifts, small groups, drama, contemporary music, financial stewardship, spiritual transformation, and more. For ordering information, call (800) 570-9812 or visit our website at www.willowcreek.com.

WCA MEMBERSHIP

Membership in the Willow Creek Association as well as attendance at WCA Conferences is for churches, ministries, and leaders who hold to a historic, orthodox understanding of biblical Christianity. The annual church membership fee of $249 provides substantial discounts for your entire team on all conferences and Willow Creek Resources, networking opportunities with other outreach-oriented churches, a bimonthly newsletter, a subscription to the *Defining Moments* monthly audio journal for leaders, and more.

To find out more about WCA membership, visit our website at www.willowcreek.com.

WILLOWNET (WWW.WILLOWCREEK.COM)

This Internet resource service provides access to hundreds of Willow Creek messages, drama scripts, songs, videos, and multimedia ideas. The system allows you to sort through these elements and download them for a fee.

Our website also provides detailed information on the Willow Creek Association, Willow Creek Community Church, WCA membership, conferences, training events, resources, and more.

WILLOWCHARTS.COM (WWW.WILLOWCHARTS.COM)

Designed for local church worship leaders and musicians, WillowCharts.com provides online access to hundreds of music charts and chart components, including choir, orchestral, and horn sections, as well as rehearsal tracks and video streaming of Willow Creek Community Church performances.

THE NET (HTTP://STUDENTMINISTRY.WILLOWCREEK.COM)

The NET is an online training and resource center designed by and for student ministry leaders. It provides an inside look at the structure, vision, and mission of prevailing student ministries from around the world. The NET gives leaders access to complete programming elements, including message outlines, dramas, small group questions, and more. An indispensable resource and networking tool for prevailing student ministry leaders!

CONTACT THE WILLOW CREEK ASSOCIATION

If you have comments or questions, or would like to find out more about WCA events or resources, please contact us:

Willow Creek Association
P.O. Box 3188, Barrington, IL 60011-3188
Phone: (800) 570-9812 or (847) 765-0070
Fax: (888) 922-0035 or (847) 765-5046
Web: www.willowcreek.com

TOUGH QUESTIONS

Garry Poole and Judson Poling

"The profound insights and candor captured in these guides will sharpen your mind, soften your heart, and inspire you and the members of your group to find vital answers together."   —Bill Hybels

This second edition of Tough Questions, designed for use in any small group setting, is ideal for use in seeker small groups. Based on more than five years of field-tested feedback, extensive revisions make this best-selling series easier to use and more appealing than ever for both participants and group leaders.

Softcover

How Does Anyone Know God Exists?	ISBN 0-310-24502-8
What Difference Does Jesus Make?	ISBN 0-310-24503-6
How Reliable Is the Bible?	ISBN 0-310-24504-4
How Could God Allow Suffering and Evil?	ISBN 0-310-24505-2
Don't All Religions Lead to God?	ISBN 0-310-24506-0
Do Science and the Bible Conflict?	ISBN 0-310-24507-9
Why Become a Christian?	ISBN 0-310-24508-7
Leader's Guide	ISBN 0-310-24509-5

Pick up a copy at your favorite local bookstore today!

WILLOW CREEK RESOURCES

ZONDERVAN™

GRAND RAPIDS, MICHIGAN 49530 USA

WWW.ZONDERVAN.COM